Collins

Social Studies for Jamaica Grade 8

Workbook

Series Editor: Farah Christian

William Collins' dream of knowledge for all began with the publication of his first book in 1819. A self-educated mill worker, he not only enriched millions of lives, but also founded a flourishing publishing house. Today, staying true to this spirit, Collins books are packed with inspiration, innovation and practical expertise. They place you at the centre of a world of possibility and give you exactly what you need to explore it.

Collins. Freedom to teach.

Published by Collins
An imprint of HarperCollins*Publishers*
The News Building, 1 London Bridge Street, London, SE1 9GF, UK

HarperCollins*Publishers*
Macken House, 39/40 Mayor Street Upper, Dublin 1, D01 C9W8, Ireland

Browse the complete Collins Caribbean catalogue at
www.collins.co.uk/caribbeanschools

ISBN 978-0-00-841400-9

British Library Cataloguing in Publication Data
A catalogue record for this publication is available from the British Library.

Publisher: Dr Elaine Higgleton
Commissioning editor: Kate Wigley
In-house senior editor: Craig Balfour
Author: Steve Eddy
Series editor: Farah Christian
Editorial project management: Oriel Square
Copyeditor: Andy Slater
Series designer: Kevin Robbins
Cover photo: © LBSimms Photography/Shutterstock
Maps: © CollinsBartholomew
Typesetter: Jouve India Pvt. Ltd.
Production controller: Lyndsey Rogers
Printed and bound by: Martins the Printers

Acknowledgements
The publishers gratefully acknowledge the permission granted to reproduce the copyright material in this book. Every effort has been made to trace copyright holders and to obtain their permission for the use of copyright material. The publishers will gladly receive any information enabling them to rectify any error or omission at the first opportunity.

Contents

Question Key

 Questions marked with a triangle test recall

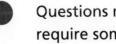 Questions marked with a circle require some critical thinking and application of facts

 Questions marked with a square require higher order thinking and analysis

 Questions marked with cogs are STEAM activities

 **Read pages 8–9 of the student book, 'What is nationalism?'.
Then answer the questions.**

a) What does a 'state' have that a 'nation' may not necessarily have?

   i) Its own political institutions

   ii) A defined territory

   iii) A single shared language

   iv) A shared culture

b) What is sovereignty?

   i) Being ruled by a king or queen

   ii) Having a national currency

   iii) A country's right to govern itself

   iv) A country's history

c) Which statement is not true of Jamaica?

   i) It is a republic.

   ii) It is a constitutional monarchy.

   iii) It is a parliamentary democracy.

   iv) It has a prime minister and a cabinet.

d) What is 'national identity'?

   i) Our ethnicity or racial identity

   ii) Any characteristics that we are born with

   iii) Jamaica's unique political system

   iv) What it means to belong to a country, state or nation

e) What is Jamaica's national motto?

   i) Live and Let Live

   ii) Out of Many, One People

   iii) All for One and One for All

   iv) Fight the Good Fight

2 Complete this paragraph using words from the word bank below.

The words 'nation' and '_____' are often used interchangeably but, strictly speaking, they are different. A _____ is a large group of people who are joined in having a shared background, culture and _____, living in a particular country or territory. A state is distinguished by having its own _____ institutions. Jamaica is a 'sovereign state' because it _____ itself. It became a _____ state in 1962. Like Britain, its head of state is the British monarch, Queen Elizabeth II, but the monarch has no real _____ or authority in Jamaica. Jamaica is a _____ democracy.

governs	language	nation	parliamentary
political	power	sovereign	state

3 Using your existing knowledge and/or research on the internet, write a paragraph explaining how Jamaica, as a nation and as a state, is different from a) the United States, and b) China.

_____

_____

_____

_____

_____

_____

4 Study the Jamaican Coat of Arms on page 9 of the student book. The government of Jamaica has asked you to design a new coat of arms with a motto. Draw it below, labelling it to explain its features, or describe it in detail so that an artist would be able to create it from the details you provide.

Explain the meaning behind the features of your design.

5 **Read pages 12–13 of the student book, 'The ideal Jamaican citizen'. Then answer the questions.**

a Tick the characteristics below that make a good or ideal Jamaican citizen.

i) Taking responsibility for your community

ii) Being law-abiding

iii) Minding your own business

iv) Voting in elections

v) Respecting the rights of others

vi) Being a high earner

vii) Helping to preserve Jamaica's cultural heritage

viii) Taking part in local and national events

ix) Supporting Jamaican sports teams

x) Protecting the environment

b Referring to the case study on page 13, select *True* or *False* for the following statements.

i) Astley Smith is a resident of Kingston. *True/False*

ii) The May Day Basic School has been named in Smith's honour. *True/False*

iii) Smith has worked to develop the Basic School for twenty years. *True/False*

iv) Each year he has helped one student to attend the University of the West Indies. *True/False*

v) He has received the Queen's Achievement Award. *True/False*

vi) He is vice-president of the citizens' association and neighbourhood watch. *True/False*

c Explain the following terms in your own words:

i) Patriotism

_____

ii) Voluntary work

_____

iii) Citizen

_____

iv) Ideal (as in 'the ideal citizen')

_____

6 **Write a paragraph explaining in what ways you are already a good Jamaican citizen, and in what ways you think you could do even better as you get older.**

_____

_____

_____

_____

_____

_____

7 **Read pages 14–15 of the student book, 'What is Vision 2030?'.**

a Fill in the gaps to list the problems facing Jamaica that Vision 2030 aims to address. Choose words from the word bank below.

i) Poor _____ growth

ii) High levels of _____ debt

iii) Unacceptable levels of _____ and poverty

iv) High levels of crime and _____

v) Low levels of skill, weak business and _____

vi) Rapid urbanisation, migration and _____ negatively affecting family life

economic	globalisation	industry
national	unemployment	violence

b Draw lines to match up the guiding principles of Vision 2030 with what they involve.

a) Social cohesion	**A.** Conserving natural resources and balancing the environment and the economy
b) Equity	**B.** Being clear and open about what is taking place
c) Transformational leadership	**C.** Getting groups and individuals to agree
d) Sustainability	**D.** Working with different groups to meet the goals
e) Sustainable development	**E.** Taking responsibility for what has already happened
f) Partnership	**F.** Making sure that individuals in society have equal opportunities
g) Transparency	**G.** Having leaders who can implement significant social changes
h) Accountability	**H.** Ensuring communities and businesses grow without harming the environment

c Research the following terms. In your own words, explain what they mean, and in what ways they could create problems in Jamaica.

Term	Meaning	Possible problems or negative effects
Urbanisation		
Migration		
Globalisation		

d Choose one problem listed in part a) that you think is particularly important. Write a paragraph explaining your choice. You might include:.

- how the problem affects you personally or your family

- how it affects people's standard of living

- how it affects the attitude of non-Jamaicans (e.g. tourists, investors) to Jamaica.

_____

_____

_____

_____

_____

_____

8 **Read pages 16–21 of the student book, 'What are the four goals of Vision 2030?'**

a Complete the four goals of the National Development Plan. Refer to page 16 if necessary.

Goal 1: Jamaicans are _____ to achieve their fullest _____.

Goal 2: The Jamaican society is _____, _____ and just.

Goal 3: Jamaica's economy is _____.

Goal 4: Jamaica has a healthy natural _____.

b Now write the six words from part a) in the left-hand column of the table below and explain what each means.

Word	Explanation

 c Design a poster to promote the four goals of Vision 2030.

Begin by thinking of four powerful and easily identifiable visual images – one to represent each goal. Then think of a single word or short phrase to sum up each goal. Use colours for impact.

Briefly describe your images here, and add the words or phrases.

Image	Word or phrase
1	
2	
3	
4	

Draw your poster below, or on a separate sheet, or provide a rough sketch, adding a detailed description that would enable an artist to create it based on your own creative vision.

9 **The next three questions focus on the individual goals of Vision 2030.**

a) Other than for Covid-19, which two other kinds of vaccination have recently been implemented as part of efforts to achieve Goal 1?

_____

_____

b) Which goal will be helped by the installation of more CCTV cameras?

_____

c) What are Wigton III and BMR Jamaica, and which two goals do they help with?

_____

_____

d) What is the name of the programme designed to help young technology entrepreneurs by providing them with skills?

_____

e) What does 'effective governance' mean in Goal 2?

_____

f) What is meant by 'a stable macro economy' in Goal 3?

_____

_____

g) What goal is benefited by the annual Coastal Clean-up Day?

_____

h) What is meant by 'hazard risk reduction' in Goal 4?

_____

_____

10 Look at the characters described in the table below. For each one, suggest one goal that they might be especially keen to see achieved. In the final column, explain why.

Character	Goal	Why
I'm Carson. I started a web design company last year. Our business is slowly growing, but we may need a loan to expand in order to compete with foreign companies.		
I'm Ronica. I have two young children, but eventually I hope to train to become a secondary school teacher. My mother lives with us, so she could help with the children, but I do worry about her health.		
I'm Deangelo. I run a late-night convenience store. I get some rowdy young men in here sometimes, and some cause trouble. More worryingly, last month the shop across the street was held up at gunpoint.		
I'm Ora. I'm very concerned about the environment generally, especially global warming. I live on the west coast, near Cousins Cove, and I hate to see the rubbish that builds up on the beach. I do my bit to clear it up every year.		
I'm Rita. My boyfriend Aaron and I are really into nature and hiking in the mountains. We've talked about starting a company organising guided tours.		

11 Imagine that it is 2030 and all Goals have been achieved. You have been working abroad for years, and now you return to Jamaica and are amazed to see how it has changed. Write to a friend describing how different it is, and why you think they should come and see for themselves. Aim to write about 200 words. Use a separate sheet of paper if necessary.

_____

_____

_____

_____

_____

12 Use AI to create pictures to show changes implemented leading up to 2030 and what their accomplishment looks like in a post-2030 Jamaica. Stick your pictures on a separate piece of paper.

13 Read pages 20–1 of the student book. Select _True_ or _False_ for the following statements.

a) Educational achievement levels of boys and girls are currently equal.
True/False

b) A major challenge to Vision 2030 is cost.
True/False

c) Parenting has a key role to play in achieving the goals of Vision 2030.
True/False

d) All Jamaican schools have 100 per cent attendance.
True/False

e) Not all Jamaican citizens trust the police.
True/False

f) There are insufficient social resources in rural areas.
True/False

g) Jamaica is not at all vulnerable to climate change.
True/False

h) Tourism in Jamaica has been hit by the Coronavirus pandemic.
True/False

14 **Look at the wordsearch below.**

a) Find eleven local challenges (within Jamaica) to the National Development Plan. Words may appear in any direction, including diagonally. Note that one of the challenges is made up of two words.

```
E  Z  O  H  Y  S  P  B  E  F  T  W  J  U  E
S  D  C  J  O  K  T  S  N  E  C  M  C  H  T
E  J  U  C  N  O  I  S  I  V  O  R  P  E  A
A  R  I  C  C  N  P  E  F  I  E  R  E  C  M
B  A  U  E  A  I  S  J  C  T  M  Q  P  O  I
L  V  E  T  R  T  P  H  R  D  P  T  R  N  L
H  W  H  B  L  C  I  A  Z  X  L  M  D  O  C
N  M  A  M  M  U  D  O  B  K  O  S  Q  M  I
S  K  P  I  R  E  C  Y  N  A  Y  C  S  I  K
H  E  A  L  T  H  C  A  R  E  M  W  E  C  L
L  E  W  V  C  W  A  X  L  X  E  N  M  C  E
G  O  V  E  R  N  A  N  C  E  N  A  I  X  T
S  E  M  I  K  I  M  M  B  M  T  H  R  V  Y
M  R  A  W  U  H  L  A  W  S  T  Y  C  U  K
E  R  U  T  C  U  R  T  S  A  R  F  N  I  R
```

b) Choose one of the challenges and, in your own words, explain why it is a challenge.

_____

_____

_____

_____

_____

_____

15 **Choose the three challenges that you think are the most important. Then write a letter to the Jamaican Prime Minister explaining why it is so important for these three challenges to be addressed.**

Begin with a short introductory paragraph. Then write one paragraph for each challenge. Then write a short concluding paragraph. Use a separate sheet of paper if necessary.

_____

_____

_____

_____

_____

_____

_____

_____

_____

_____

_____

_____

16 **Read page 21 of the student book.**

a) Complete the paragraph using words from the word bank.

Coronavirus has meant that the Jamaican _____ has had to review the goals of Vision 2030. Economies all over the world are suffering, so Jamaica is receiving less _____, and there is reduced global demand for Jamaican _____. There has obviously been less _____ too, because non-essential travel has been impossible. Coronavirus has had a _____ impact on Goal 3 of Vision 2030. However, there has been good _____ with Goal 1: 'Jamaicans are Empowered to Achieve their Fullest Potential'.

exports	government	investment
negative	progress	tourism

b) In 2016/17, what percentage of Goal 3 targets were met?

   i) 10%

   ii) 73%

   iii) 46%

c) In 2015, progress in reducing levels of crime and violence was:

   i) outstanding.

   ii) almost non-existent.

   iii) on target.

d) For Goal 1, there has been a reduction in the:

   i) child mortality rate.

   ii) literacy rate.

   iii) level of school absenteeism.

17 **Read pages 22–3 of the student book, 'What is national development?'.**

   a What three things does national development include?

   _____

   _____

   _____

   b Explain how each of the following would benefit the Jamaican economy.

   i) Good education for all.

   _____

   _____

   ii) An efficient and affordable transport system

   _____

   _____

   iii) Medical care for all

   _____

   _____

c In the table below explain the possible benefits to society of these individual behaviour choices.

Choices	Benefits
Buying sustainable goods, e.g. recycled paper or fairtrade goods	
Using renewable energy sources	
Getting involved with activities benefiting the community	
Recycling goods	
Using public transport, cycling or walking	
Volunteering for organisations that help people in need or protect the environment	

d Tick the choices you have ever made yourself.

1 **Read pages 30–1 of the student book, 'Communication'.**

Sort the scrambled key terms in the table below into their correct forms.
Then briefly explain each one in your own words.

Scrambled word	Correct word	Your explanation
toomuncimanic		
befadeck		
miaed		
duemim		
nol-narbve		
verrecie		
neerds		
rebval		

2 **Complete the following paragraph using words from the word bank.**

Communication is about the transfer of _____. We can communicate
in words or gestures, through _____ such as company logos, and via
different _____, such as telephone, _____ or Zoom. A modern
_____ needs up-to-date computer _____ and employees who
are trained to use it. The _____ makes instant global _____
possible, providing the _____ is fast and reliable.

business	communication	connection
email	information	internet
media	symbols	technology

3 In the table below, draw or describe your own ideas for symbols for the items listed.

Item	Symbol
Warning: children playing on street	
Danger of electric shock	
Drinks and snacks available	
Safe drinking water	
Warning: wet floor	
Hiking route in National Park	

4 Explain why there is sometimes an advantage in using signs and symbols rather than words.

_____

_____

_____

_____

_____

_____

5 Read pages 32–3 of the student book, 'Technology'. Draw lines to link each keyword with its correct definition.

Keyword		Definition
Technology		Book-size electronic device with applications similar to a laptop or smartphone
Internet café		Electronic book
Communication technology		Place where the public can pay to access the internet
Smartphone		Experience of receiving too much information to process
Tablet		Information transfer between sender and receiver using technology
Ebook		Inactive, mostly sitting
Sedentary		Devices and systems created for practical purposes and to make work more efficient
Information overload		Mobile phone that runs applications like a small computer; it has internet access and can take photos

6 Answer these questions about internet usage.

a In 2020, what percentage of the world's population did not use the internet to communicate or research?

_____

b By what percentage did global internet use increase between 1994 and 2020?

_____

c In 2020, the population of the world was 7.8 billion. A billion is a thousand million. How many million people worldwide used the internet in 2020?

_____

7 **Answer these questions about technology in the future.**

a) Write a paragraph describing what changes in communications technology you expect to have taken place by 2040.

_____

_____

_____

_____

_____

_____

b) Imagine yourself 50 years from now. Write a paragraph comparing technology then with how it was back in your teens. For example, you might write, 'If people back then wanted to communicate with someone a long way away, they had to use a so-called 'smartphone' that they had to carry around with them. Imagine – they had no access to…'

_____

_____

_____

_____

_____

_____

_____

8 **Read pages 34–7 of the student book about mass media.**

a) Name two types of print media.

_____   _____

b) Name two devices that use digital media.

_____   _____

c) What name is given to the type of media including TV and radio?

_____

d) What kind of media includes Facebook, Instagram and X?

_____

 9 **Focus on 'Who has access to information?' and the 'Did you know?' on page 34.**

a) What percentage of the Jamaican population did not access the internet in 2023?

_____

b) By what percentage did people accessing the internet increase each year from 2017 to 2023? Give your answer to the nearest whole number.

_____

c) How many women in Jamaica used Facebook Messenger in October 2019?

_____

d) By what percentage did the number of Facebook Messenger users _fall_ between February and March 2019?

_____

 10 **Tick the main reasons for Jamaicans _not_ using the internet.**

a) Too busy

b) Cannot afford device or access

c) Disability

d) Lack of technological skill or confidence

e) Religious objections

f) Illiteracy

g) Prefer to read books

 11 **Complete the table below showing the standards of 'quality journalism'.**

Descriptive term	What it means
Balance	
	Acknowledging errors and correcting them
Truthfulness/accuracy	
	Putting the interests of the public (what benefits them) above other interests
Fairness	

12 What would be the primary purpose of each of these examples of mass media?

a) A film set in America's Wild West.

_____

b) A televised speech by the Prime Minister about why we should be proud to be Jamaican.

_____

c) A website telling people about endangered turtles and what people can do to save them.

_____

13 List one way that social media could have been used by government or social agencies to influence change among the people who used it during that time.

_____

_____

14 Write a bullet-point plan for an essay comparing the advantages and disadvantages of mass media.

_____

_____

_____

_____

_____

_____

15 Read pages 38–9 of the student book, 'Do you always know the intent?' Tick either Fact or Opinion for each of these statements.

Statement	Fact	Opinion
A. Jamaica is a great country to live in.		
B. Jamaica is a parliamentary democracy.		
C. School attendance is compulsory in Jamaica.		
D. Maths is more important than history.		
E. Jerk chicken is a popular dish.		
F. The voting age should be lowered to 16.		

16 Explain how each of the following uses emotive language (makes an emotional appeal).

Example	Your explanation
A. The proposed motorway will rip a devastating gash through this fragile ecosystem.	
B. Don't let housework rule your life. Discover freedom with the new Breeze vacuum cleaning system. Breeze? Yes please!	
C. Guys – do you lack confidence, feel inferior, find it hard to get noticed? Try Rocko, the protein drink that's guaranteed to build muscle in weeks.	
D. Crime is a disease and no one is immune. Vote RSP to reclaim the streets!	

17 In your opinion, what is the biggest problem facing Jamaica today? Write a paragraph explaining your views. Support your argument with at least one piece of evidence. Say what you think should be done about this problem.

_____

_____

_____

_____

_____

_____

_____

_____

18 Read pages 40–1 of the student book, 'What messages are being transmitted through the media?'.

a) What do you understand by the word 'stereotype'?

_____

b) Name three different types of stereotyping in the media.

_____

_____

_____

c) Name one way in which adverts might encourage gender stereotypes.

_____

19 Read pages 42–3 of the student book, 'What is social media?'.

a Tick the names below that refer to social media platforms.

A. Snapchat   **B.** Facebook

C. Google   **D.** X

E. MyFace   **F.** Instagram

G. Messenger   **H.** LinkedIn

b Choose three of the social media platforms you ticked in part a). Imagine you have a friend or older relative who has never used social media. Write a brief summary explaining to them how each of your three platforms can be used.

Platform	How used
1	
2	
3	

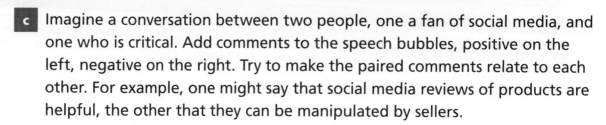

c Imagine a conversation between two people, one a fan of social media, and one who is critical. Add comments to the speech bubbles, positive on the left, negative on the right. Try to make the paired comments relate to each other. For example, one might say that social media reviews of products are helpful, the other that they can be manipulated by sellers.

Facebook groups can be a great way for people with shared interests or concerns to exchange information.

20 Read pages 46–7 of the student book, 'Responsible use of social media'.
Select *True* or *False* for the following statements.

a) Research shows that TV has no effect on children's ability to focus and complete tasks.
True/False

b) Experts advise against sharing passwords with anyone other than your parents.
True/False

c) Social media platforms automatically block cyberbullying.
True/False

d) There are no laws in Jamaica to prevent online crime.
True/False

e) It is a good idea to take breaks from social media, and to turn it off a short time before you go to bed.
True/False

f) If you delete a photo that you have posted online, it is automatically deleted throughout the internet, and on any devices to which it has been downloaded.
True/False

1 Read pages 54–5 of the student book, 'Remembering what is meant by culture, heritage and ancestors'. Unscramble the key words for this unit below, and draw lines to match them to the definitions.

Scrambled	Key word
acronsets	
amstingrim	
eagerhit	
ecrutul	
lucilatutrumi	
ulrulcat	

Definition
Such things as religion, language, beliefs, traditions and heritage
Cultural features created in the past which continue to be important in a society
Made up of several cultural groups
People from whom we are descended
Relating to culture
People from one country coming to live in another one

2 The things listed below are examples of which elements of Jamaican heritage? For example, one element is 'cuisine'. Add an example of your own for each heritage element.

Example	Element of heritage	Your own example
Bandannas		
Brother Anansi		
Reggae		
Jerked chicken		
The Blue Mountains		
The Jamaica Carnival		

3 You have been asked to assist with designing a brochure for visitors to Jamaica telling them what elements of cultural heritage they can expect to encounter here. On a separate sheet, outline the information that will be included in the brochure. Then write brief notes for the designer about three or four pictures that you would like to include in the leaflet.

4 Read the text under the heading 'Ancestors' on page 55 and look at the pie chart. Then select *True* or *False* for the following statements.

a) All people living in the Caribbean share the same ancestors.
True/False

b) The first people who lived in the Caribbean were Amerindians.
True/False

c) Most people in the Caribbean have African cultural backgrounds.
True/False

d) Ten per cent of the Caribbean population is white.
True/False

e) Less than 1 per cent of the Caribbean population is of Hispanic descent.
True/False

5 Reread the 'Ancestors' text. Then read the following passage and fill in the gaps using the word bank below.

The Caribbean is a _____ region, meaning that its people embrace many different cultures. The _____ of the present population came from many different countries and cultures. For example, in Jamaica some are descended from the _____ who were the first to _____ the Caribbean islands. However, they only make up 0.9 per cent of the Caribbean _____, which is the same proportion as that made up by those of _____ descent. The majority of people are of _____ descent. After this come those of _____ descent, and third come those whose ancestors were _____. These different groups brought different _____, with their different festivals and _____, as well as the different _____ in which they spoke.

| African Amerindians ancestors ceremonies Hispanic Indian |
| inhabit languages mixed multicultural population religions |

29

6 Read pages 56–7 of the student book, 'What are the elements of a culture?'. Read this account of a Jamaican teenager's life. Identify what elements of culture she refers to by underlining a sentence, key word or phrase and adding a number 1–9 to match the aspects of culture outlined on page 56.

Hello. My name is Cedella and I'm 15. I live in Portmore with my parents, grandmother and older brother Aston. My father works in a warehouse in Kingston, and my mother in a supermarket in Portmore. We live in a bungalow with a veranda, so we can sit outside in the shade on a hot day. My parents left school in their teens, but I want to go to college and study science. At home I speak Patois with my parents, and especially my granny, but at school I mostly speak English.

My parents are members of the Church of God, so we go to church on Sundays. My brother doesn't always go now because he prefers to play football. He also trains as a sprinter. I'm more into music, like dancehall and new reggae. I listen to Koffee a lot. She got famous by recording a tribute to Usain Bolt. My father says her music is not his idea of reggae – he prefers Bob Marley and Peter Tosh.

My grandma is still a great cook, and she's teaching me to make her speciality dish – ackee and codfish (saltfish).

I'm glad that we live in a democracy, and I intend to vote as soon as I'm old enough. I'm also glad that the police are trying to work with the community, and that they are answerable to the government.

7 Now write an account of how your own life and values are different from, or similar to, Cedella's. Alternatively, use a smartphone or tablet to film yourself giving an account.

_____

_____

_____

_____

_____

_____

_____

8 Read pages 58–9 of the student book, 'What is a cultural icon?'. The following could be called cultural icons of various countries. Conduct research on the internet to find out about them and what countries they are associated with. What would you say are possible Jamaican equivalents?

Cultural icon	Country	Jamaican equivalent
a) The Stars and Stripes flag		
b) The kangaroo		
c) The Leaning Tower of Pisa		
d) William Shakespeare		
e) Abraham Lincoln		
f) The Beatles		
g) Niagara Falls		
h) Diego Maradona		
i) Muhammad Ali		
j) Joan of Arc		
k) The lotus flower		
l) Rosa Parks		

9 You found an article on the internet about the Hope Botanical Gardens (see page 59 of the student book). Unfortunately it contains ten factual errors. See if you can spot them and correct them.

The Hope Botanical Gardens are the largest public green space in Jamaica. They contain many common species of plants and trees, including the Hibiscus elatus (purple mahoe), the nation's national flower.

The gardens, established in 1973, are also known as the Royal Floral Gardens. A beautiful Jamaican landmark, they include 100 acres of land in the Barbican area of St Andrew.

The gardens were created on land within the estate of Colonel Richard Hope, one of the original Spanish colonisers.

10 Read pages 60–1 of the student book, 'What are the criteria for accepting persons as cultural icons?'. Then answer these multiple choice questions.

a) Which of these is least likely to be considered a cultural icon?

   i. A musician   **ii.** A plate of food

   iii. A mountain   **iv.** A politician

b) Which of these traits is *not* necessary in order for someone to become a cultural icon?

   i. They must have contributed to the country's cultural and national development.

   ii. They must have become very rich.

   iii. They must have enhanced Jamaica's international image.

   iv. They must have made achievements through hard work and dedication.

c) Which of these is *not* a Jamaican cultural icon?

   i. Michael Norman Manley   **ii.** Usain Bolt

   iii. Dr Thomas Lecky   **iv.** Toussaint L'Ouverture

11 Choose three people mentioned in this section. Explain in your own words why each of them is a cultural icon. Use a separate sheet if necessary.

Cultural icon	Why a cultural icon?
1	
2	
3	

12 Bearing in mind what this section says about cultural icons, choose five other possible icons and explain why you think they deserve to be regarded as such. At least two of these should be people. Use Word or PowerPoint with images of the icons.

13 Read pages 62–3 of the student book, 'Cultural Identity'.

a) Name three things that could be connected to Jamaican national identity.

_____

_____

_____

b) Name three things that are part of any individual's cultural identity.

_____

_____

_____

c) Name three things that might make you feel proud to be Jamaican if you were visiting another country and were asked about your background.

_____

_____

_____

d) Name three things that you think you would have in common with another Jamaican that you met abroad.

_____

_____

_____

14 Referring to page 63, 'Caribbean identity', write a paragraph describing how far you believe you share an identity with people from other Caribbean islands. You could refer to similarities and differences. For example, you may feel that some things are uniquely Jamaican.

_____

_____

_____

_____

_____

_____

_____

15 Read pages 64–5 of the student book, 'Significant historical events that have shaped Jamaican culture'. Select *True* or *False* for the following statements.

a) Hurricane Gilbert was a Jamaican boxer who never lost a fight.
True/False

b) There has not yet been a female Jamaican Prime Minister.
True/False

c) Jamaica had been inhabited for about 1000 years when Columbus arrived.
True/False

d) Slave revolt leader Sam Sharpe was pardoned.
True/False

e) Thirty years passed between the Slave Trade Abolition Bill and Emancipation.
True/False

16 Number the events in the table below in their chronological order 1–7 and add their dates.

Event	Order	Date
A Slave revolt leading to Maroon war		
B Jamaica Labour Party (JLP) founded		
C Columbus arrives and claims Jamaica for Spain		
D Jamaica's first female Prime Minister		
E Emancipation of enslaved people		
F Slave trade Abolition Bill		
G Maroon treaty signed with Nanny		

17 From the timeline, aided by research online, briefly explain why each of the following people was significant in Jamaica's history.

Person	Significance
a) Portia Simpson-Miller	
b) Christopher Columbus	
c) Nanny	
d) Tacky	
e) Sam Sharpe	
f) Paul Bogle	
g) Marcus Garvey	

18 Read pages 66–7 of the student book, 'Political icons in Jamaica'.

a) When was the Order of National Hero established?

_____

b) How many people have received the honour of National Hero so far?

_____

c) Which icon led the Maroons?

_____

d) Which icon founded the Universal Negro Improvement Association in 1914?

_____

e) Which icon led a march on a courthouse?

_____

19 Match the political icons with the details by writing the correct letter in the middle column next to the icon's name.

Political icon		Detail
a) Paul Bogle		A Led the Christmas Rebellion
b) Sir Alexander Bustamante		B Fought a war 1720–39
c) Marcus Garvey		C Founded the PNP
d) George William Gordon		D Led a protest march on a courthouse
e) Norman Manley		E Founded the JLP
f) Queen Nanny		F Sold his land to freed slaves
g) Samuel Sharpe		G Founded the PPP
h) Sir Howard Cooke		H Jamaica's fifth PM
i) Edward Seaga		I Knighted in 1994

20 Write a paragraph about why Jamaica needs political icons or national heroes.

_____

_____

_____

_____

_____

_____

_____

21 Read pages 68–73 of the student book, 'Jamaican cultural icons and their contributions'. Then complete the crossword.

Across	
2.	Prize won by Marlon James
5.	Dance that has three styles
8.	Bob Marley's type of music
10.	Novel by Claude McKay
11.	Author of Black Leopard
12.	Nickname of Shelley-Ann Fraser-Pryce
14.	Hit single by Marcia Griffiths
15.	Famous reggae band

Down	
1.	Jamaican language
3.	Dancer and choreographer
4.	Sprinter who won at three Olympics
6.	Sculpture by Laura Facey Cooper
7.	Co-founder of National Dance Theatre Co.
9.	Burru and Tambu are examples
13.	Film with Louise Bennett-Coverley

22 Write one or two paragraphs about what aspects of Jamaican culture you enjoy.

_____

_____

_____

_____

_____

_____

_____

_____

_____

_____

23 Read pages 74–5 of the student book, 'Global recognition' and answer the questions.

a) What type of music is The Mighty Sparrow known for?

i) Reggae

ii) Calypso

iii) Mento

iv) Rock

b) What is Courtenay Bartholomew known for?

i) Medical research

ii) Cricket

iii) Economics

iv) Art

c) Who designed the opening ceremonies of the 1992 and 1996 Olympics?

i) Eric Williams

ii) Toots Hibbert

iii) Lee Perry

iv) Peter Minshall

4 The Caribbean Landscape and Its Influence on Human Activities

1 Read pages 84–5 of the student book, 'Types of rock'. Then complete the table of key terms and definitions.

Key term	Definition
Cementation	
	The weight of sediment squeezing down on a previous layer
Deposited	
	Formed on the Earth's surface
Igneous	
	Formed inside the Earth
Metamorphic	
	Aggregate of minerals forming part of the Earth's crust
Sedimentary	
	Mineral substance on the Earth's surface which sustains plants
Solidified	
	Physical features of an area
Transported	

2 Complete the passage below using the words in the word bank.

Rock is a _____ material exposed on the surface of the Earth or lying beneath the _____ which is the upper layer of the Earth in which plants grow. Topography refers to either the _____ of the land surface or the study of it.

There are three main types of rock. The most common, _____, is formed when magma from the Earth's _____ rises and cools. It can be formed above ground (_____) or below (_____). Sedimentary rocks form when layers of mud or silt at the bottom of the _____ are compressed by later layers lying on top of them. Metamorphic rocks are formed when igneous or _____ rocks become heated or _____ underground.

extrusive	igneous	intrusive	mantle	mineral
pressurised	sea	sedimentary	shape	soil

3 Choose examples of three types of rock (e.g. marble) – one igneous, one sedimentary, and one metamorphic from the examples given in the student book.

a) Research and make notes on how each one is commonly used.

Type of rock	Example	How is it used?
Igneous		
Sedimentary		
Metamorphic		

b) Look at the picture of a fossil on page 85 of the student book. Research and make notes on how fossils are formed. Then write one or more paragraphs on this process to be included in a children's encyclopaedia.

_____

_____

_____

_____

_____

_____

_____

_____

_____

4 Read pages 86–9 of the student book, 'The topography of the Caribbean'. Match Column A to the correct ending in Column B.

Column A	Column B
a) Mountainous areas in Jamaica	a sedimentary rock
b) Coastal plains are found around	bauxite mining companies
c) There are active volcanoes in	are metamorphic rocks
d) The beaches of Negril and Grand Anse	are covered with dense evergreen rainforests
e) Igneous rocks include	Dominica, St Vincent and St Lucia
f) Marble, schist and serpentinite	granite, gabbro, pegmatite and basalt
g) Limestone is	inaccessible parts of Jamaica
h) Cockpit Country is one of the most	home to the Flower Bat and the Fig-Eating Bat
i) Karst is a type of landscape that is	have fine-textured white sands nearly 11km long
j) Caves often contain	of aluminium
k) Marta Tick Cave is	particularly found in limestone areas
l) Karstic hazards include	the edges of the hills and mountains
m) Bauxite is the main raw ingredient	seasonal drought and flooding
n) Alcan and Alcoa are	stalagmites and stalactites

5 Complete these words relating to topography using the clues given.

a) Staying in leaf throughout the year   _ v _ _ g _ _ _ n

b) Opening at the top of a volcano   _ r _ _ _ _ r

c) Type of sedimentary rock   _ i _ e_ _ _ n _

d) Limestone landscape   k _ _ _ _ _

e) Hole in limestone where water drains away   _ _ _ k h _ _ e

f) Ground sinking or collapsing   _ u _ _ _ d e _ _ _ _

g) Mineral mined in Jamaica   _ _ _ x _ t _

6 You are starting a company to provide holiday and tour packages in the Caribbean to people who love geology. On a separate sheet of paper, write the text of a webpage describing what interesting topographical features your clients can expect to see. Appeal to them directly. For example, you could begin, 'If you love geology and want a fascinating Caribbean holiday, why not…'

7 Compare the geological map on page 87 with a map of Jamaica (e.g. on Google Maps) and answer these questions.

a) Identify where you live in Jamaica. What type of rock can be found where you live or closest to where you live?

_____

b) What kind of rock would you find in the central and eastern Blue Mountains?

_____

c) If you travelled from Kingston to Oracabessa (north coast), what kind of rock would you mostly be crossing?

_____

d) What kinds of rock would you find around Morant Bay?

_____

8 Read pages 90–1 of the student book, 'Physical landforms and features in the Caribbean'. Select *True* or *False* for the following statements.

a) The Rio Minho is the longest Caribbean river.
True/False

b) Jamaica's longest beach is Seven Mile beach, near Negril.
True/False

c) Jamaica's highest peak is in the Blue Mountains.
True/False

d) May Day mountains is in Manchester parish.
True/False

e) Jamaica's central mountain chains are made of sedimentary rock.
True/False

4

The Caribbean Landscape and Its Influence on Human Activities (cont.)

9 Unscramble the words for topographical features in the table below, using the clues to help you. Then write sentences explaining what each word means.

Scrambled	Clue	Your sentence
yab	Good place to drop anchor	
cheab	You might want to lie around on it	
epac	Sticks out	
elinstoac	Jamaica's is 248 km long	
stainonum	Good viewpoints	
thoum	Go downstream and you'll get here in the end	
errive	Jamaica's longest is almost 100 km	
course	Go upstream and you'll get here in the end!	

10 Using the map and table on page 91, mark the five highest peaks in Jamaica on the outline map below. Number them in order of height.

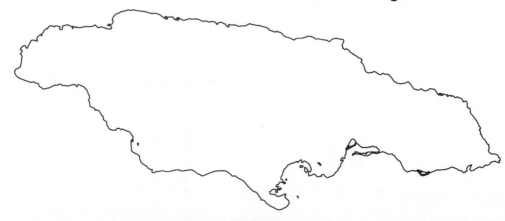

11 Read pages 92–5 of the student book, 'Land use in Jamaica'.

a) Name the four main different sizes of settlement.

_____

_____

_____

_____

b) Name four different products of agriculture.

_____

_____

_____

_____

c) Name the three types of settlement pattern.

_____

_____

_____

12 Jamaica has three officially recognised cities: Kingston, Portmore and Montego Bay.

a) Mark these cities, together with Spanish Town, Mandeville and May Pen, on the blank outline map below.

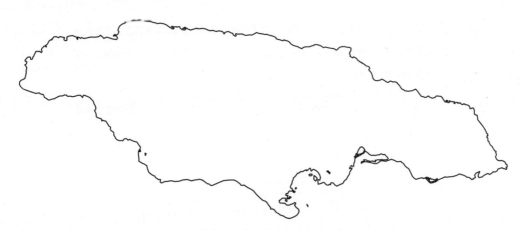

b) Using the internet, research the population size of each settlement. Write these populations on the map.

4

The Caribbean Landscape and Its Influence on Human Activities (cont.)
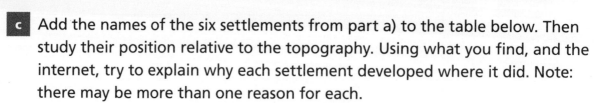

c Add the names of the six settlements from part a) to the table below. Then study their position relative to the topography. Using what you find, and the internet, try to explain why each settlement developed where it did. Note: there may be more than one reason for each.

Settlement	Reasons for development

13 Using Google Maps satellite view, and/or your own knowledge, find at least one example of each of the three settlement types. List them here with their name, type and location.

Name	Type	Location

14 Answer these questions about services.

a) Give an example of a low-order service.

_____

b) What order of service (low, middle or high) do you think a nail salon is?

_____

c) What kind of facility is Montego Bay Sports Complex?

_____

15 Read the paragraph below. Where a scrambled word or phrase (from the Key vocabulary on page 95 of the student book) appears, write the unscrambled version in the space provided.

In rural areas you may find either **levistokc** _____ or **berala marfing** _____ _____, but in towns and cities there are more **visceres** _____, such as schools, hospitals and banks. In cities, especially, you are likely to find a range of **inertcoarlea** _____ **setalicifi** _____, such as gyms, swimming pools and art galleries. Travel is also easier because of the **osmonicaoctium** _____ network.

You will probably not find **maripry dusitriens** _____ _____ in a city centre, and even **condesary** _____ ones manufacturing things like cement and paper are more likely to be on the outskirts. However, many at the **retiatry** _____ level, such as banking and retail, are located in city centres.

16 Draw a map of your area showing some of its facilities, its communications (roads/railways that connect to other areas), land use or where activities and services are located. If you live in a rural area, use arrows with distances to show how far the nearest facilities are. Complete your map with a title, key and direction point. Use a separate sheet of paper if necessary.

4

The Caribbean Landscape and Its Influence on Human Activities (cont.)

17 Read pages 96–9 of the student book, 'Population distribution and density' and 'Choropleth dot maps'. Match the key terms below to their definitions.

Key term	Definition
a) population	map showing population density using shading
b) census	number of people living in an area
c) population density	towns and cities
d) population distribution	average number of people living in 1 square km
e) urban areas	villages, hamlets, countryside
f) rural areas	how population is spread out
g) choropleth map	map showing population density and distribution using dots
h) dot map	method of gathering population data

18 Refer to the 'Did you know...?' on page 96.

a) Which CARICOM member has the largest population?_____

b) Which has the smallest population?_____

c) Which is the closest to Jamaica in terms of population size?

_____

19 Look at the map on page 98 of the student book. Also find a political world map in your atlas and compare the two.

a) Which is more densely populated, India or Australia?_____

b) Which is more densely populated, the USA or Canada?_____

c) In what country is the densely populated island north of Australia?

_____

20 Look at the dot map on page 99.

a) What is the population of Trelawny Parish in thousands?_____

b) What is the most densely populated parish?_____

c) What is the second most densely populated parish?_____

21 Read pages 100–1 of the student book, 'Relief and settlement; population distribution in Jamaica'. Complete the paragraph below using words from the word bank.

Mountainous areas in Jamaica are _____ populated because the land is difficult to _____ on, not suited to _____, and may be prone to _____. Some hilly areas are densely forested, making _____ difficult. Swamps and _____, usually found near the coast, are almost impossible to build on. Other _____ areas are densely populated because they are relatively _____.

agriculture	build	coastal	flat
landslides	marshes	settlement	sparsely

22 Read pages 102–3 of the student book, 'Relief and settlement in the Caribbean'. Look at the calculation on page 102. There are 273 people in each square kilometre of Jamaica, so you could work out its population by multiplying this by its size in kilometres. The area of Cuba is approximately 110 000 square kilometres and its density is 102, so what is its population?

_____

23 Look at the table on page 102.

a) Which is the second most densely populated Caribbean country?

_____

b) Which is the second most sparsely populated Caribbean country?

_____

24 Use the space below to draw a bar chart showing the relative densities of the four most densely populated Caribbean countries. Label it with their names.

4

The Caribbean Landscape and Its Influence on Human Activities (cont.)

25 Read pages 104–7 of the student book, 'Relief and economic activities and communication'. In the context of topography, what is 'relief'? Tick the correct answer.

a) Coastal indentations

b) Land height and contours

c) A variation in an otherwise monotonous landscape

d) The network of river drainage

26 What three economic activities are influenced by relief in Jamaica?

_____

_____

_____

_____

27 Referring to the agriculture map on page 104 and the parishes map on page 101, answer these questions.

a) Which parish mostly grows citrus fruits?

_____

b) What is the only crop grown in Trelawny as a main crop?

_____

c) In which parish are bananas and coconuts grown as the only main crops?

_____

d) Which parish only has sugar cane and livestock farming?

_____

e) Which parish grows every type of crop except coconuts but has very little livestock?

_____

28 On a separate sheet, describe how you could make a 3D model of Jamaica showing how relief influences tourism.

29 Study the industry map on page 106 and answer the questions.

a) Where are the two main industrial areas?

_____   _____

b) What are two main ports for bauxite?

_____   _____

c) Where is there an oil refinery? _____

d) Which parish has three separate bauxite mining areas?

_____

e) What are the industries in St Thomas parish?

_____

f) Explain why the alumina plants in St Elizabeth and Manchester parishes are located where they are.

_____

g) Name one major port for shipping bananas_____

h) What is the major port for shipping sugar?_____

i) Why do you think several sugar refineries are located close to rum distilleries?

_____

30 Refer to page 107.

a) What relief feature influenced the route of the Junction roadway between Kingston and the north coast?

_____

b) Why do roads often run along the coast?

_____

c) Why do roads sometimes leave the coast and run inland?

_____

d) Why are there few roads in the Blue Mountains and Cockpit Country?

_____

31 Read pages 108–11 of the student book and complete the crossword of key concepts.

Across	
1.	Reduction of land's fertility or appeal
5.	Has made rivers dry up
7.	Creates wealth but scars landscape
9.	Hillside farming method to reduce erosion
10.	Safeguarding

Down	
2.	Condition caused by reduced rainfall
3.	Reuse to reduce environmental impact
4.	Contamination, e.g. by bauxite
6.	Replanting of trees
8.	Soil being carried away, usually by water

32 Read pages 112–15 of the student book. Complete the passage below using words from the word bank.

A map gives a _____ of the landscape from above – a _____ view. A map of a room or building is called a _____ plan.

A map is drawn to _____, so that we can assess distances in real life by comparing them with the much smaller distances on the map. Scale is one of the _____ of map-making (_____). Another is that a map usually has the direction _____ at the top. There is also normally a _____, also called a key, which shows what each _____ represents. For example, a cross might be used to represent a church.

Map-makers (_____) design different types of map to show different _____. A road map focuses on route planning. A _____ map shows rock types.

bird's-eye	cartographers	cartography	conventions
floor	geological	information	legend
north	scale	symbol	view

33 In the space below, or on a separate sheet of paper, create a map of a 100 square metre area with your home at its centre. Decide on any symbols, labelling and colour-coding you will need.

 34 Read 116–21 in the student book. Answer these questions.

a) Which of the maps on page 116 has the largest scale?_____

b) Which shows more detail, a large-scale map, or a small-scale one?

_____

c) A map drawn to the scale 1:100 000 would show a distance of 1 km (1000 m) as 1 cm on the map. How many centimetres on the map would represent 5 km?

_____

d) What scale would the map have to be to represent 1 km by 10 cm?

_____

e) Which shows more detail, a 1:25 000 or a 1:50 000 map?_____

35 The map of Jamaica below is drawn to a scale of 1:2 000 000. Use the grid to draw a map of Jamaica to the scale of 1:4 000 000.

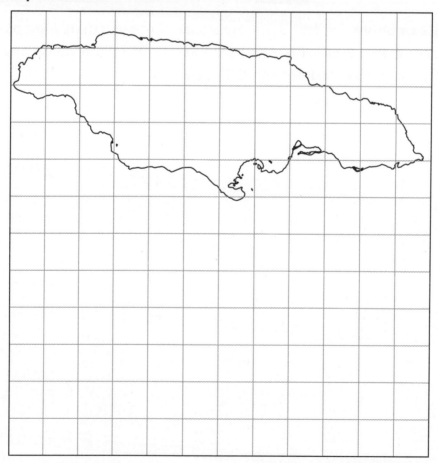

36 Read pages 122–7 of the student book. Complete each sentence by circling the correct option.

a) On a map, an arrow pointing towards the letter N is showing the position/ **point/longitude/direction** north.

b) A magnetic **compass/barometer/meridian/locator** points towards the magnetic north.

c) The imaginary line around the Earth that is equidistant from the North and South poles is called the **meridian/equator/equaliser/ecuador**.

d) The four main directions are the **primary/quadratic/cardinal/linear** points.

e) Northeast is a **secondary/intermediate/indeterminate/tertiary** point.

f) The vertical lines of the grid squares dividing up a map are the **hustings/ northings/eastings/gridlings**.

g) The horizontal lines on a grid are the **northings/flatlines/westings/zonals**.

37 Look at the map on page 124 and read page 125. In which squares are the following?

a) Hanover parish   _____

b) St Ann parish   _____

c) Kingston   _____

d) Portland Point   _____

38 Read page 126. Use the table below to compare the advantages and disadvantages of conventional paper maps and electronic maps that you might use on a smartphone.

	Advantages	Disadvantages
Paper map		
Digital		

1 Read pages 134–7 of the student book.

a) Categorise each of the following into a type of institution.

i) A building society _____

ii) An orphanage _____

iii) A local council _____

iv) A prison _____

b) Which two institutions might provide help with your homework?

_____   _____

2 Remind yourself of the activity on page 134 of the student book. Imagine that you are in a group of fifty people on the island. Make notes in the table below on the advantages and disadvantages of different forms of decision-making.

	Advantages	Disadvantages
People vote for a number of representatives, who vote on issues, e.g. where to build shelters.		
People vote for a leader, who then makes all the rules.		
Everyone votes on each issue.		
The strongest individual takes control.		
There are no leaders or rules, but people can choose to co-operate with others if they wish.		

3 **Read pages 138–141 of the student book.**

a) Explain why a country usually uses a standard currency rather than allowing all currencies to be used.

_____

_____

b) Suggest what one advantage and one disadvantage would be if we were to use lead bars as currency instead of paper money.

_____

_____

c) If a government wants to fund new social enterprises, what would be the problem with it simply printing more money to pay for them?

_____

_____

d) Some peoples in the past have used cowrie shells (seashells) as money. What would the advantages and disadvantages of this be?

_____

_____

e) People in the past have used barter – reaching an agreement on the exchange of goods (e.g. I give you a donkey and you make me a table). What might the advantages and disadvantages be?

_____   _____

f) Give one example of a need and one of a want.

_____

_____

g) Give one advantage and one disadvantage of saving money under your mattress.

_____

_____

h) What two kinds of need for money are served if I invest in a company, but I know that I can cash in some of my shares if I need to buy a new car?

_____   _____

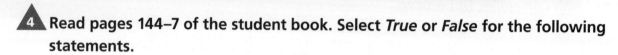

4 Read pages 144–7 of the student book. Select *True* or *False* for the following statements.

a) A credit union is owned by its own members. *True/False*

b) The first Jamaican credit union was formed in 1993. *True/False*

c) The basis of a credit union is that its members help each other. *True/False*

d) The more investment a member has in the credit union, the more power they have in its decision-making. *True/False*

e) Credit unions only do business with their own members. *True/False*

f) Any profit made by a credit union goes to its president. *True/False*

g) The JCCUL has over 1.5 million members. *True/False*

5 Select the correct option.

a) A regulated financial institution is one that:

  i)   has limited funds.

  ii) operates within rules and laws set by the government.

  iii) guarantees a regular income to its investors.

  iv) is controlled by a foreign government.

b) A partner plan is a savings plan that:

  i)   provides for the surviving partner or spouse in the event of one partner's death.

  ii) spreads risk by linking two separate savings companies.

  iii) is backed by the government.

  iv) requires members to pay into a fund from which they eventually benefit.

c) A job in the informal economy is one in which:

  i)   there is no need to dress smartly.

  ii) the worker may not pay taxes and will not receive a pension.

  iii) one involving information technology.

  iv) one based on supplying incriminating evidence to the police.

6 Read pages 148–9 of the student book, 'The role of economic institutions'. The table below shows functions of public and private economic institutions. Tick a box to divide the functions into public and private.

	Public	Private
a) Provide financial assistance to other institutions		
b) Make opportunities to set up businesses and create employment		
c) Protect public funds		
d) Offer loans, e.g. for house purchase		
e) Ensure that financial transactions are transparent and legal		
f) Offer goods and services to satisfy individual needs and wants		
g) Offer employment opportunities		
h) Ensure that the national economy is stable		
i) Collect taxes		

7 Which cybercrime is described in each case?

a) The criminal demands payment to unfreeze a computer system.

_____

b) Someone's personal details are stolen, so that the criminal could digitally impersonate the victim.

_____

c) The criminal sends an email claiming to be from a recognised institution, such as PayPal, inviting the recipient to click on a link, which will install malware or trick them into parting with money or bank details.

_____

d) The criminal hacks accounts to access users' login details, which they may also have used for other websites.

_____

8 Carry out research and write a paragraph on how individuals can guard against cybercrime. Write your answer on a separate sheet of paper.

9 Read pages 150–3 of the student book. Tick which of these you think is sensible advice on budgeting.

a) Add up your regular income so you know what you can expect.

b) Add up your savings.

c) Make a list of friends you could borrow money from.

d) Work out your essential spending, e.g. rent/mortgage, bills, fares, food, clothes.

e) Take more risks: sooner or later you're sure to get lucky.

f) Work out the gap between your income and spending.

g) Aim for zero spending.

h) Be honest about how you spend on needs.

i) If you have debts, try not to think about them.

10 Unscramble these words relating to financial planning and match them to the definitions.

Scrambled word	Unscrambled	Match	Definition
a) tenixdeprue			i) a loan secured on a property (especially a home)
b) emocin			ii) long-term plan to support you in retirement
c) batsility			iii) a sustainable financial state
d) vennorispdeg			iv) amount you spend
e) gagtrome			v) describing what is left of income after essentials have been paid for
f) lasyra			vi) exceeding what you can afford
g) asisdeplob			vii) itemised financial plan
h) niosnep			viii) money coming in
i) tebd			ix) owing money
j) tegbud			x) regular money paid to an employee

11 Plan a story about what happens when someone fails to plan financially. Write the story on a separate sheet of paper.

6 Consumer Affairs

1 Read pages 160–1 of the student book, 'Key concepts in understanding consumer affairs'. Fill in the blanks in the passage from the word bank.

A _____ is anyone who spends money on _____, such as food or clothing, or _____ like dry cleaning or taxi hire. We can distinguish between our _____, such as shelter, food and water, and our _____, such as a TV or smartphone. Many things fall somewhere in between. For example, we need clothes to keep us warm, but we may buy new, _____ clothes before our old ones have worn out, because we want to _____.

Our society could be called a consumer society because the _____ is driven by people spending money on things they want. Companies selling _____ or services pay for _____, which uses _____ to persuade us that we need them. If we use a _____ card to buy them, and do not pay it off each month, then we are consuming credit.

advertising	consumer	credit	economy
fashionable	goods	impress	needs
products	psychology	services	wants

2 In the table below, list eight goods or services you have consumed recently. You may have paid for them yourself, or someone else may have done. They could also be something you share with others, like a TV. Give each one a score 1–5 depending on whether they are a need or a want, with 1 being an essential need and 5 being a pure luxury – a want.

Item consumed	Score 1–5

3 Read pages 160–3 of the student book. How do you relate to the factors listed in the table on page 162? Give your own examples in the table below.

Factor	How you relate to it
Consumers' tastes and preferences	Think of something you used to like and/or buy that you no longer want or like. (Maybe it has gone out of fashion.)
Consumers' income	Think of an item you would buy if you had more money.
Changes in the price of goods	Think of something you buy now but would no longer buy if its price increased significantly.
Advertising	Think of an advert that may have influenced you.
Market size	What is there that you think a lot more people might buy if they knew more about it. (Or you could suggest a new product.)
Quality of goods or services	What do you have that you think works so well that you would buy it again, or buy other goods from the same company?

4 On a separate sheet, list three adverts from any medium, e.g. on TV, on a billboard, or online, that you think are effective. For each one say:

- what it is advertising (e.g. a drink, a chocolate bar, a car)

- who do you think it is aimed at (e.g. teenage girls)

- how it works to persuade consumers to buy the product or service.

5 **Read pages 166–7 of the student book, 'Rights and responsibilities of the consumer'. Which of these people have had their consumer rights violated? Explain your decisions. Bear in mind:**

- which right(s) may have been violated

- whether the buyer has in any way failed in their own responsibilities

- what you think the fair outcome should be.

Case	Violated?	Your explanation
Dorcas bought an iPhone in the market at a very good price. When she tried to register it with Apple, the ID number was not recognised. Also, when she put it on charge overnight, it heated up and almost caused a fire.		
Marlon bought some new trainers, but he was in a hurry, so didn't try them on. When he wore them on a date with his new girlfriend, he found they were tight and uncomfortable. He wants his money back.		
Celine paid a bakery in advance to make her parents a wedding anniversary cake with their names in icing. But the bakery got confused with another order and put 'Gloria' on it instead of 'Marcia'.		
Noel bought some fish salad and ate it for lunch that day. That afternoon he got sick. When he read the label, he saw it was three days after its 'Use by' date.		

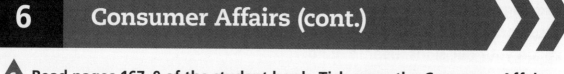

6 Read pages 167–9 of the student book. Tick areas the Consumer Affairs Commission (CAC) includes in its education programme.

a) Budgeting and shopping hints

b) Food safety

c) Recipes and menu suggestions

d) Where to go on holiday

e) Environmental matters

f) Advice on colour schemes for decorators

g) Consumer rights

h) Dieting

7 Select *True* or *False*.

a) The CAC provides market research information. *True/False*

b) The CAC gives presentations to schools. *True/False*

c) The CAC runs a free dating agency. *True/False*

d) The CAC offers complaints resolution. *True/False*

e) The OUR regulates utility companies, including those for water, sewage and electricity. *True/False*

f) The Bureau of Standards Jamaica encourages standardisation of goods, processes and practices. *True/False*

g) The National Consumers' League has campaigned on Genetically Modified Foods and Intellectual Property Rights. *True/False*

h) The NCL encourages Jamaicans to consume as much as they possibly can. *True/False*

8 Read pages 172–7 of the student book. Tick what you consider to be advantages of globalisation.

a) Companies do business with suppliers and customers across the world.

b) If countries profit from each other, they may be less likely to go to war.

c) Manufacturers can import raw materials worldwide.

d) Individuals can interact with others worldwide through social media.

e) Cities worldwide increasingly have the same food outlets, e.g. McDonalds.

f) Big corporations can use tax loopholes to pay less tax.

g) We are able to enjoy food from all across the world.

h) We can eat imported fruit and vegetables that are not in season in our own country.

i) There are employment opportunities abroad, including for those who cannot find jobs at home.

j) People no longer need to buy locally produced goods.

9 Refer to the above list.

a Write a paragraph about how any one or two of these things could have both advantages and disadvantages.

_____

_____

_____

_____

_____

_____

b On a separate sheet, write one or two paragraphs about the advantages and disadvantages of globalisation. Do these advantages and disadvantages balance each other out? If you like, focus on a few of the factors in part a)

10 Imagine you work for a big internet technology company. Create a PowerPoint plan using bullet points for a speech to a trade commission on how important the internet is to modern business and how you see it becoming even more important in the future.

11 **Answer the following questions.**

a) What does the 'e' stand for in e-commerce?

_____

b) What is a 'virtual' store?

_____

c) Why is it a good idea to use a credit card for online payments?

_____

d) Why should you use different passwords for different websites?

_____

12 **Tick which of the following you would personally go online to find or buy, assuming you had the money to do so.**

a) A novel

b) A holiday abroad

c) A ready-cooked pizza

d) A puppy

e) A pack of T-shirts

f) Postage for a parcel

g) A new partner

h) Music

i) Petrol

j) A weekly supermarket shop

k) Shoes

l) Handmade jewellery

13 **Outline plans for an e-commerce platform or marketplace for Jamaica which allows people to recycle and reduces the negative effects of consumerism.**

_____

_____

_____

_____

14 **Referring to some of your choices in activity 13, write one or two paragraphs on the advantages, disadvantages and limitations of internet shopping. Use a separate piece of paper.**

1 Read pages 186–8 of the student book. Complete this crossword.

Across	
4.	Bodily effect of cold
5.	Measure of heat
8.	Set of atmospheric conditions at a time and place
10.	Damp
11.	Tropical wet climate
12.	Needs tropical climate and seasonal rainfall

Down	
1.	Requires tropical wet climate
2.	Tropical storm with circulating wind pattern
3.	Weather pattern in one place over time
6.	Spinning column of air
7.	Caribbean's type of climate zone
9.	Cyclone moving faster than 33m per second

2 Write a paragraph about how the weather affects your daily life, what you wear, and your mood. For example, do you go to the beach? Do you wear shorts or an overcoat? Do you feel happier if it is hot and sunny, or do you prefer some shade and a cool breeze?

_____

_____

_____

_____

_____

_____

3 Fill in these weather details for the area you live in today.

Current temperature _____

Highest temperature today _____

Lowest temperature today _____

Current wind speed and direction _____

Rain or chance of rain _____

4 Read page 189 of the student book. Imagine you are a farmer living in a particular part of Jamaica who grows one or more crops. (The map on page 104 of the student book may help.) Write two diary entries for different times of the year giving details of what work you are doing and how it is affected by the weather or climate. Carry out research into weather or climate conditions required for particular crops if necessary.

_____

_____

_____

_____

_____

_____

5 Read pages 189–90 of the student book, 'Climate graphs'.

    a) Which is the driest month in Montego Bay?_____

    b) When and where does rainfall exceed 200 mm?

    _____

    c) Which of the three places shown has the least rainfall in January?

    _____

    d) What do you notice about temperatures in Negril from June to October?

    _____

6 Look for rainfall and temperature information and maps of different places online. Find areas with:

    a) high annual rainfall and high temperature _____

    b) high annual rainfall and low temperature _____

    c) low annual rainfall and high temperature _____

    d) low annual rainfall and low temperature _____

7 Research online to find current weather conditions for the following places and give a brief description of conditions in each place.

    a) Timbuktu, Mali _____

    _____

    b) Quaanaaq, Greenland _____

    _____

    c) Furnace Creek, USA _____

    _____

    d) Glasgow, UK _____

    _____

8 Look up the places in activity 7 in Google satellite view. On a separate sheet of paper, write a paragraph in which you imagine yourself visiting one of these places.

- Describe the weather on the day you visit.
- Find out about the climate of the place and its effects on people there.

9 **Read pages 192–3 of the student book, 'Climate change and global warming: causes'.**

Create a flow chart showing the causes and effects of climate change by putting the factors listed in the word bank in the correct boxes and adding further words of your own, if you wish. You could also add your own images to make the chart more visual.

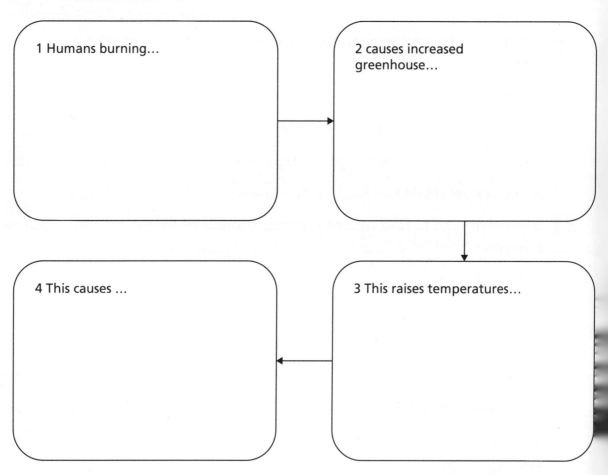

1 Humans burning…

2 causes increased greenhouse…

4 This causes …

3 This raises temperatures…

oil	increases rainfall	creates drought		greenhouse effect
nitrous oxide	gas	ice caps	gases	polar	deforestation
fossil fuels	coal	vehicles	carbon dioxide	flooding
heat waves	crops	warmth is trapped		methane
	planes	emissions		

10 Select *True* or *False*.

a) Climate change has happened naturally in the past.
True/False

b) Carbon dioxide, methane and nitrous oxide are the main greenhouse gases.
True/False

c) Coral reefs are endangered by global warming.
True/False

d) Climate change only affects a few low-lying islands.
True/False

e) Climate change causes more rain in some areas and less rain in others.
True/False

f) Melting polar ice caps are raising sea levels.
True/False

g) Global warming increases the number of hurricanes.
True/False

11 Read pages 194–5 of the student book, 'Human activities and climate change'. Summarise the ways in which the following human activities contribute to climate change.

a) Travel

_____

_____

b) Agriculture

_____

_____

c) Deforestation (for timber or to clear land)

_____

_____

d) Industry

_____

_____

12 Imagine you are developing policies for a new Jamaican political party focusing on stopping climate change. You are going to design an election flyer. Use the template below.

Think of a name for your party

Punchy paragraph explaining why your party is needed

Photo brief

Add 6–10 bullet points outlining your environmental policies (p181 of the student book will help)

---

13 Read pages 196–9 of the student book, 'The effects of climate change', and complete the sentences using the word bank.

a) Carbon dioxide dissolves into the sea, causing increased _____

b) Rising sea levels are caused by melting _____.

c) Acidification reduces marine life's ability to extract _____ carbonate for shells and skeletons.

d) Extreme weather events such as _____ have caused deaths and devastation in the Caribbean.

e) The transformation of fertile land into an arid or semi-arid region is called _____.

f) Deforestation causes _____, impoverished soil, and an increase in carbon dioxide, which creates global warming

g) In 2012, Hurricane Sandy caused millions of dollars' worth of _____.

h) When sea temperatures rise, corals expel their algae, resulting in coral _____.

i) Coral reefs are natural _____ that absorb the force of waves and storm surges.

j) The death of coral reefs damages fishing and _____, as well as whole ecosystems.

tourism	hurricanes	glaciers	erosion	desertification
damage	calcium	bleaching	barriers	acidification

14 Use the information in activity 13 to help you write a paragraph warning of the effects of climate change in the Caribbean.

_____

_____

_____

_____

_____

_____

_____

15 Read pages 200–1 of the student book, 'Organisations which manage and monitor climate change'.

a) Which agreement seeks to limit the rise of the global temperature below 2° Celsius?

   i) Warsaw Agreement

   ii) New York Agreement

   iii) London Agreement

   iv) Paris Agreement

b) Which agreement was made in Japan in 1997?

   i) Kyoto Protocol

   ii) Geneva Convention

   iii) Treaty of Utrecht

   iv) The Fourth Protocol

c) What does IPCC stand for?

   i) International Progress Caribbean Council

   ii) Internal Performance Climate Council

   iii) Intergovernmental Panel on Climate Change

   iv) Intelligent Panel for Climate Care

d) When was the Climate Change Division established in Jamaica?

   i) 1870   ii) 2012

   iii) 2021   iv) 1994

16 Research the aim of one of these international environment conventions. Use what you find out to plan an education campaign on a separate piece of paper. Your campaign should inform the public and the industries responsible for environmental harm. Be sure to include traditional and social media platforms. You could include slogans, posters, comic strips, brochures, songs and adverts.

17 Read pages 202–5 of the student book. Complete the speech bubbles to show which R each of these people is addressing? Add the keyword.

1 Tyrone:
I throw my potato peelings onto the compost for my granddad's vegetable garden.
R _____

2 Irie:
I go to a community shop where I can pay to refill my laundry liquid bottle instead of buying a new one.
R _____

3 Winston:
I take used bottles and jars to the bottle bank so they don't just go to landfill.
R _____

4 Gabrielle:
I try to repair things whenever I can instead of just throwing away and buying new.
R _____

5 Leroy:
I save money and help the environment by asking, before I buy something, whether I really need it.
R _____

18 Add simple images and either a ✔ or a ✘ to each of them to complete this poster design. Refer to page 203 of the student book for your information.

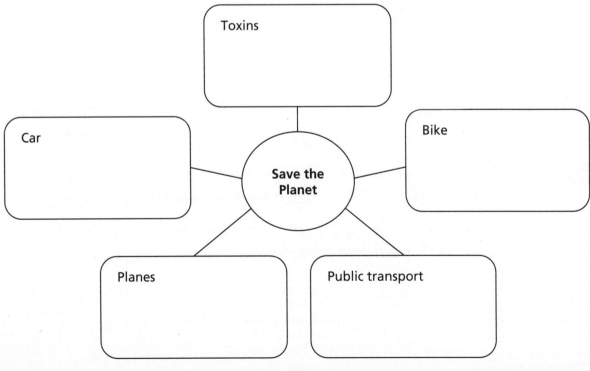

19 **Complete the water-saving advice by referring to page 203 of the student book.**

a) When brushing your teeth _____

b) Take shorter _____

c) Don't flush garbage _____

d) Avoid soaps _____

e) Choose reusable or refillable products, not _____

20 **Summarise the information about eating on page 204 of the student book in no more than three sentences.**

_____

_____

_____

_____

21 **Answer the following questions.**

a) Why should we cut our use of fossil fuels?

_____

_____

b) What alternatives are there to fossil fuels?

_____

_____

22 **If you were going to mount a campaign to get people to do just three of the things listed on page 205 of the student book, which three would you choose?**

Base your choice on how easily you could persuade people and what the benefits would be. Explain your choices below

_____

_____

_____

1 Complete the table below referring to page 212 of the student book and the Glossary.

Key term	Definition
	A naturally caused major adverse event
Hazard	
	Giant wave moving fast across the sea's surface
Eruption	
	Mountain from which lava, gas, steam and ash sometimes burst
Oil spill	
	Catastrophe caused by human activity
Flood	
	Destructive spinning column of air

 2 Read the case study on page 213 of the student book. Imagine you are a journalist and you have just attended a press conference on the day of the oil spill. Use the template below to write your report. Record it on your smartphone or tablet as a TV news feature.

What has happened, where and who is involved (or what company)?

What damage has occurred so far? Include a statement from Petrojam.

What damage is feared? Include a statement from an environmental group.

What and when was Jamaica's first major oil spill?

3 Read pages 214–17 of the student book. Complete this crossword using key vocabulary from these pages.

Across	
2.	Huge section of rock beneath Earth's surface
4.	Wet soil moving suddenly downhill
6.	Scale showing earthquake strength
8.	Size of earthquake
10.	Relating to movement of tectonic plates
12.	On surface directly above earthquake's focus
13.	Where an earthquake happens underground

Down	
1.	Sudden downhill movement of rock and earth
3.	Twelve-point scale measuring intensity
5.	Sudden shaking of Earth's crust
7.	Referring to plates beneath Earth's surface
9.	Smaller earthquake following main one
10.	Instrument to measure ground movement
11.	Level of effects caused by earthquake

4 Complete the paragraph using words from the word bank.

Earthquakes happen when tectonic _____ move. They happen at plate _____ (margins). At _____ plate margins, plates are moving _____ from each other. At _____ plate boundaries, an _____ plate and a continental plate are moving towards each other. At _____ plate margins, the plates are _____ past each other. At continental _____ plate boundaries, two continental plates are moving _____ each other.

> towards   sliding   plates   oceanic   destructive
>
> constructive   conservative   collision   boundaries   away

5 Look at the map on page 214 of the student book. Answer these questions.

a) Which two Caribbean countries are in the zone of 'Frequent strong earthquakes'?

_____   _____

b) When was the last major earthquake in Jamaica?

_____

c) Where in the Caribbean was there a major earthquake in 2010?

_____

6 Read the case study on page 217.

a) How far from the capital was the epicentre of the 2010 earthquake?

_____

b) What other country was affected?

_____

c) Haiti lies on the boundary of which two tectonic plates?

_____   _____

d) Why did emergency services have difficulty in reaching many areas?

_____

e) How long did the aftershocks go on for?

_____

f) How high were the tsunami waves?

_____

7 Read pages 218–21 of the student book.

a) Which of these is not an essential to stock up on in case of earthquake?

i) Food

ii) Water

iii) Magazines

iv) Medical supplies

b) Which of these is *not* a key word in a worldwide earthquake strategy?

i) Drop

ii) Run

iii) Hold

iv) Cover

c) What are buildings built to withstand earthquakes designed to be?

i) Flexible

ii) Rigid

iii) Lightweight

iv) Cheap

d) How much warning is it possible to give of an earthquake?

i) About 45 minutes

ii) A few seconds

iii) 3–4 days

iv) Ten minutes

8 For each reminder word, list tasks to be completed if there is an earthquake.

Reminder	Task
Aware	
Procedures	
Services	
Reassurance	
First-aid	
Accounting	
Others	
Order	

9   Read pages 222–5 of the student book.

a Circle the ten key vocabulary words from these pages in the puzzle below.

```
M  E  O  H  I  V  M  A  L  O  D  C  R  N
O  P  I  V  O  Y  S  C  A  A  O  L  P  E
S  P  S  V  N  T  C  F  H  W  R  D  Y  I
O  I  V  N  A  A  O  L  A  W  Y  L  R  S
A  D  Y  S  C  D  A  I  R  C  O  E  O  R
V  L  I  L  L  W  E  A  R  O  O  I  C  Y
I  T  O  D  O  I  T  A  H  M  L  H  L  O
S  T  R  S  V  L  Y  E  T  P  O  S  A  S
C  D  O  R  M  A  N  T  H  O  E  I  S  F
O  T  H  A  C  T  I  V  E  S  I  R  T  L
S  E  X  T  I  N  C  T  O  I  O  N  I  O
I  S  S  T  D  I  C  T  I  T  O  Y  C  W
T  I  W  E  A  T  M  A  S  E  C  V  V  N
Y  E  T  T  C  O  O  O  E  N  R  R  W  C
```

b Add the words to the correct meanings below.

Key word	Meaning
	Forming as tectonic plates move away from each other
	Still likely to erupt
	Downhill movement of hot gas and ash
	Will probably never erupt again
	Consisting of hot gas and ash
	Flowing mix of water and volcanic ash and debris
	Degree of thickness in lava
	Mountain from which lava, gases and ash sometimes burst
	Type of volcano forming at destructive plate boundaries
	Has not erupted for a long time, but may still do so

10 Look at the map on page 222 of the student book.

a) Which two Caribbean countries have active volcanoes?

_____

b) Which is the most northern extinct volcano in the Caribbean?

_____

c) How many dormant volcanoes does Dominica have?

_____

d) In what state is Qualibou, St Lucia (active, dormant, extinct)?

_____

11 Complete the paragraph using words from the word bank.

Molten rock below ground is known as _____. Once it is above ground it is known as _____. This can be of low or high _____. Volcanic _____ is coarser and harder than wood ash, and does not dissolve in _____. A volcanic _____ is a chunk of rock ejected from a volcano during an _____. Gases ejected from a volcano include _____ dioxide, sulphur _____ and hydrogen sulphide, which is the most _____.

water	viscosity	toxic	magma	lava
eruption	dioxide	carbon	bomb	ash

12 Read pages 226–7 of the student book, 'The negative effects of volcanoes'. Then imagine that you have witnessed a volcanic eruption. Describe the spectacular sights and destruction that you see, using some of the key terms. Describe how you manage to escape. Continue on a separate sheet if necessary.

_____

_____

_____

_____

13 Read pages 228–9 of the student book, 'The positive effects of volcanoes'.

a) Which two of these are positive effects of volcanoes?

   i) They are a source of hydrogen sulphide.

   ii) They attract tourism.

   iii) They are a source of geothermal energy.

   iv) They prevent droughts.

b) Which two of these volcanoes are in Italy?

   i) Vesuvius

   ii) Kilauea

   iii) Etna

   iv) Montagne Pelée

c) Which two of these countries were created as a result of volcanic activity?

   i) Iceland

   ii) Haiti

   iii) Belgium

   iv) Hawaii

14 Imagine you run an Icelandic holiday company. Carry out research online for a brochure giving information on important and interesting volcanic and geothermal features. Make notes below. You could begin with the Blue Lagoon (see page 228 of the student book).

15 Read pages 230–1 of the student book, 'Understanding hurricanes'.

a) How fast does a tropical cyclone have to move to be called a hurricane?

i) 119 km per hour

ii) 60 miles per hour

iii) 10 m per second

iv) 75 m per second

b) What temperature, in degrees Celsius, does the sea have to reach for a tropical storm to start?

i) 10   **ii)** 73

iii) 38   **iv)** 27

c) What is the typical diameter, in km, of the eye of a hurricane?

i) 10–15   **ii)** 30–50

iii) 90–120   **iv)** 50–60

d) How many categories are there in the Saffir–Simpson scale?

i) 10   **ii)** 12

iii) 5   **iv)** 7

e) What is the immediate cause of a hurricane's spinning motion?

i) Warm air and moisture rise, with more air being sucked into the gap.

ii) Pockets of air of different temperatures create instability.

iii) Very high tides crash into oncoming currents, cooling the air overhead.

iv) Steam from the heated sea is whipped round by rapid changes in wind direction.

f) At what level on the Saffir–Simpson scale would you expect to see serious coastal flooding?

i) 2   **ii)** 3

iii) 4   **iv)** 5

16 Read pages 232–3 of the student book, 'Hurricanes in the Caribbean'.
Complete the paragraph using words from the word bank.

A wind of 120 km per hour or more is designated a _____. Hurricanes
used to be named after the saints' days on which they _____. Now
they are given names in _____ order. Since 1979 _____ have
alternated the _____ of names. Names of particularly _____
hurricanes, like Katrina, do not get _____. Recent major hurricanes
in the Caribbean include _____ (1988), _____ (2004) and
_____ (2012).

Sandy	reused	occurred	meteorologists	Ivan
hurricane	Gilbert	gender	devastating	alphabetical

17 Read pages 234–5 of the student book, 'Passage of a hurricane'.

a) What happens to air pressure and temperature as a hurricane approaches?

_____

b) What happens to winds as a hurricane approaches?

_____

c) What level of rainfall is there at the eye wall of a hurricane?

_____

d) Where in a hurricane would you find calm, sunny and dry conditions?

_____

e) Where in a hurricane do winds reach their strongest force?

_____

18 Research a recent Caribbean hurricane. Record its key details below.

Name and date: Area(s) affected: Top wind speed:

_____   _____   _____

Damage caused: Fatalities:

_____   _____

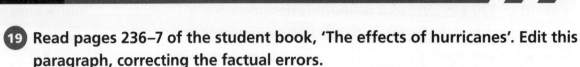
19 **Read pages 236–7 of the student book, 'The effects of hurricanes'. Edit this paragraph, correcting the factual errors.**

Hurricanes can cause hundreds of dollars' worth of damage. Often the most destructive effect is a storm surge, caused as strong winds push waves away from the coast.

In 2005 Hurricane Karina produced an 18.5 m surge – the highest ever recorded in the USA. The whole of New Orleans was under water which was 6 cm deep in places.

In 2004 Hurricane John destroyed 50 per cent of Granada's buildings, 90 per cent of its farms, 73 out of 75 schools were damaged, and 80 per cent of its power was lost. Farmland was also destroyed, but no crops were lost.

Hurricane Dora in 1963 was particularly devastating, causing damage costing $9 million and taking 7193 lives.

The amount of damage and number of deaths is in direct proportion to the category of hurricane.

20 **Read pages 238–9 of the student book, 'Preparing for a hurricane'. Select *True* or *False* for the following statements.**

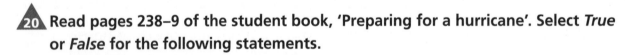

a) There is ample room in a hurricane shelter, so you can take whatever you want. *True/False*

b) A torch is a useful thing to have in a disaster supply kit. *True/False*

c) Clips can make a roof more storm resistant. *True/False*

d) If a hurricane is coming, it is best not to tell children, so as not to panic them. *True/False*

e) Deep foundations make a building more hurricane-proof. *True/False*

f) No insurance company will cover hurricane loss as it is seen as an 'act of God'. *True/False*

g) Satellites can be used to track hurricanes and warn of their impending arrival. *True/False*

21 Read pages 240–3 of the student book, 'Understanding flooding and droughts'. Tick which of these is a cause of flooding. Add 'N' to those that are natural causes, and an 'H' to those caused by human activity.

Agriculture		Climate change	
Compacted or dry soil		Deforestation	
Fishing		Golf courses	
Heavy rainfall		Impermeable rock	
Inadequate drainage		Long periods of rain	
Mining		Silting of rivers	
Snowmelt		Steep slopes	
Tourism		Urbanisation – concrete is impermeable	
Very wet, saturated soils		Trees	

22 Tick which three of these are types of drought.

a) methodological

b) meteorological

c) hypothetical

d) asymptomatic

e) hydrological

f) agricultural

g) sebaceous

23 Write out the three types of drought and explain them briefly.

_____

_____

_____

24 Complete these sentences based on 'secondary impacts' on page 242 of the student book.

a)	Water restrictions…
b)	Wildfires…
c)	Creeks…
d)	Erosion…
e)	Soil quality…
f)	Farmers are forced…
g)	Governments must …
h)	Food must be…
i)	Food prices…
j)	Tourism…

25 Read the list of flooding mitigation strategies on page 243. Explain what you think would be the difficulties or disadvantages of three of these.

_____

_____

_____

_____

26 Read pages 244–5 of the student book, 'Institutions and organisations that manage and monitor disaster preparedness'.

a) What does CDEMA stand for?

_____

b) What are the aims of the CDEMA?

_____

c) What event led to the formation of ODIPERC in 1980?_____

d) What does NEMO stand for?

_____

e) What are NEMO's disaster management programme's four phases?

_____   _____

_____   _____

27 Look at page 245 and write a summary of the WHO's aims.

_____

_____

_____

_____

28 Research the WHO from its website and other sources. On a separate sheet, write one or more paragraphs about it. You could consider:

- How it came into being
- Why it is important
- How it is run
- Its role in the Covid-19 pandemic.

1 Read pages 252–3 of the student book, 'Key concepts and components of an ecosystem', and complete this crossword including its key terms.

Across	
2.	How water runs away
6.	Life cannot exist without it
8.	Non-living
10.	Temperature and rainfall
11.	Decomposes soil
12.	Property of water altered by pollution
13.	Type of eco-friendly energy
14.	Contains nutrients that support plants

Down	
1.	Plant life
3.	In water
4.	Animal life
5.	On land
7.	Living things interacting in nature
9.	Living
10.	Grows into an aquatic ecosystem

 2 Read pages 254–7 and complete the table below to explain the key terms.

Key term	Meaning
	Short for biological diversity
biological diversity	
	Diversity of ecosystems
ecological site	
	All the elements of biodiversity that we inherit
ecology	
	Living organisms living and interacting in a specific environment
genetic diversity	
	Native to a particular region or country
indigenous fauna	
	Native plants
physical heritage	
	Variety of different species

3 Research either the Blue and John Crow Mountains National Park or Cockpit Country. Write one or more paragraphs about one of these explaining why it is so valuable as a diverse natural environment and what you would expect to find there. Continue on another sheet of paper if necessary..

_____

_____

_____

_____

_____

_____

_____

_____

_____

_____

4 Read the speech bubbles. Tick which of these people is a good ecotourist.

A. The rainforest is so beautiful and unspoilt. Let's keep to the path to keep it that way.

B. Just chuck your rubbish under a bush. We're never going to come back here.

C. I brought my own food from Kingston. I don't trust local food. We can dump the empty tins and plastic bottles in the forest. No point taking them home!

D. We stocked up on snacks in the last village before the trail. It's all good local produce.

E. We'd better follow this diversion avoiding the eroded section of the path. It's longer, but it'll cause less damage.

F. I've learned so much about the forest ecosystem from the park rangers, and from observing it first-hand.

G. Don't tell the guide, but I'm going to smuggle a couple of these rare orchids in my rucksack and sell them to a garden centre!

H. I'm taking photos of these flowers because I'm studying the cloud forest, but I certainly wouldn't pick any.

5 Read pages 258–9 of the student book, 'Flora: plants and flowers'. Complete the paragraph below using words from the word bank.

There are several reasons for the great _____ of Jamaica's flora. As an _____, it is isolated, so plants have _____ in unique ways. High _____ produces tall trees like the Lignum Vitae, and the _____ creates an environment for other types of _____. Many plants thrive in the warm, wet _____ climate. Seasonal flooding and _____ periods in the _____ suits plants that need _____ for only part of the year.

| diversity | dry | evolved | island | rainfall |
| rainforest | savannah | tropical | vegetation | water |

6 **Read page 260 of the student book.**

a How many species of birds does Jamaica have? _____

b Using a calculator, work out what percentage of Jamaica's bird species:

i) are endemic (unique to Jamaica) _____

ii) have been introduced by humans _____

iii) are considered rare. _____

c Produce a pie chart to show the proportions of endemic and introduced birds.

d Imagine you are a keen bird-watcher. Write one or more paragraphs about why Jamaica is home to so many bird species, and what birds you have seen on a holiday there. On a separate sheet, draw or paint a picture of one or more Jamaican birds.

_____

_____

_____

_____

_____

_____

_____

_____

_____

7 Read pages 261–2 of the student book.

a) Which of these is not a mammal?

i) Mongoose

ii) Manatee

iii) Turtle

iv) Whale

b) What is the one native Jamaican land mammal?

i) Mongoose

ii) Coney

iii) Bush baby

iv) Fox

c) What is the biggest threat to the manatee?

i) Whales

ii) Entanglement in fishing nets

iii) Trophy hunting

iv) Loss of habitat

d) Which of these is not a reptile?

i) Tree frog

ii) Jamaican boa

iii) Tortoise

iv) Crocodile

e) Which Jamaican species was thought to be extinct until 1948?

i) Orangutan

ii) Flightless hummingbird

iii) Iguana

iv) Tree frog

8 Read the case study on page 263. Imagine you are a *zoologist* (studying animals), an *ornithologist* (studying birds), or a *botanist* (studying plants). In the space below, make notes for an account like that of Adrian Hoskins of your visit to Jamaica. Write the full account on a separate sheet of paper.

9 Read pages 264–5 of the student book, 'our wetlands'. Sort these sentences into functions of wetlands. Add any punctuation needed.

	Scrambled sentence	Correct version
a)	acting as fish for many nurseries of species	
b)	water and cleaning storing	
c)	collecting land doesn't it flood the floodwater so	
d)	hurricanes buffer against creating storms and protecting a high tides	
e)	animals birds and other habitats providing for	
f)	depend on people providing who resources for a wetland livelihoods	
g)	and tourism pleasure recreation	
h)	mangroves prevent trees such as erosion wetland	

10 Write an action plan for a conservation organisation on what should be done to save Jamaica's mangrove swamps and why they are important. Include:

- Why they are worth saving.
- How they are threatened.
- What needs to be done.

_____

_____

_____

_____

_____

_____

_____

11 Read pages 266–7 of the student book, 'Our forests'.
Select *True* or *False* for these statements.

a) In 2018 it was calculated that forests cover 99 per cent of Jamaica. *True/False*

b) The slopes of the Blue Mountains are forested. *True/False*

c) Mahogany, balata, palms, poui and immortelle are all species of tree.
   True/False

d) Trees make soil erosion worse. *True/False*

e) Trees give out oxygen. *True/False*

f) Trees give out nitrogen oxide and carbon monoxide. *True/False*

g) Trees are important to some fish. *True/False*

h) The temperature in a forest is much higher than in surrounding areas.
   True/False

12 Use a smartphone or tablet to make a video about the importance of trees in Jamaica. Consider:

- their role in the environment
- the habitats they provide
- their importance to tourism

13 Read pages 268–9 of the student book, 'Coastal areas and waterfalls'.

a) What are known as 'the rainforests of the sea'?

_____

b) What are carite, croakers and bechine?

_____

c) Which is higher, Dunn's River Falls or Reggae Falls?

_____

d) How do people normally get up to YS Falls?

_____

14 On a separate sheet of paper, describe a visit to a Jamaican waterfall.

15 Read pages 270–1 of the student book, 'Threats to our natural heritage/ecosystems'.

a) Where is Jamaica's largest natural forest?

_____

b) What percentage of Western Jamaica's water needs are met by rivers within Cockpit Country?

_____

c) What mineral do mining companies want to mine in Cockpit Country?

_____

d) What do the Giant Swallowtail Butterfly, the Hawksbill Turtle and the Jamaican Iguana all have in common?

_____

16 Imagine an environmentalist and a mining executive exchange views on proposed mining in Cockpit Country. In the speech bubbles below, fill in what they might say. The first two have been filled in for you.

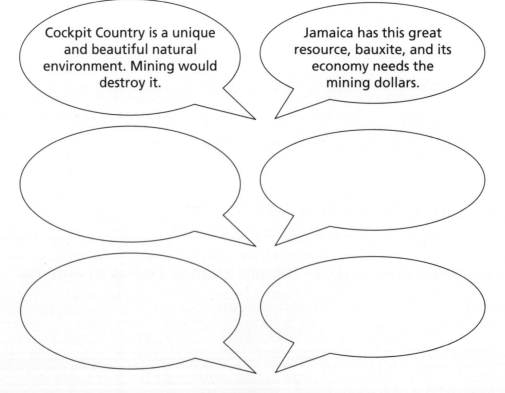

17 On a separate sheet of paper, write a paragraph expressing your own views on what should happen to Cockpit Country.

18 Read page 272 of the student book. Add the concepts to the explanations.

Concept	Explanation
	Managing natural resources such as fossil fuels or forests so that they do not all get used up.
	A policy of maintaining natural resources, such as trees, by replacing them when they are used.
	Protecting special environments with strict laws to prevent them from being damaged.

19 Read pages 274–5 of the student book, 'The role of the Jamaican government in managing the environment'.

a) What does NEPA stand for?

_____

b) Put NEPA's mission statement briefly in your own words.

_____

_____

20 Match NEPA's roles to their explanations. Write the correct letter in the middle column.

1 Environmental Management		A. Encouraging individuals and businesses to obey environmental protection laws and making sure they are prosecuted for breaking them
2 Planning		B. Informing the public about the need to protect the environment, and explaining how it is being done
3 Compliance and Enforcement		C. Managing and protecting the environment
4 Public Education		D. Producing new laws and policies, and monitoring their effectiveness
5 Policy and Research		E. Overseeing building plans to minimise impact on the natural environment

21 Research either the Forestry Department or the Water Resources Authority. Then write a paragraph about why their work is vital to Jamaica. Write your answer on a separate sheet of paper.

22 Read pages 276–7 of the student book, 'The value of conservation and preservation'.

a) In your own words, explain the difference between conservation and preservation.

_____

_____

_____

_____

b) How do you think the Jamaican government should balance the need to conserve and preserve the natural environment with the need to exploit Jamaica's resources? For example, do you think the natural environment should be preserved exactly as it is? Or should Jamaica's resources, like bauxite, be exploited as much as possible – especially because of Covid's economic impact? Explain your views.

_____

_____

_____

_____

_____

_____

_____

_____

_____

c) Make a video to explain how far you think sustainable tourism is possible and desirable in Jamaica – for example in Cockpit Country or the Blue and John Crow Mountains.

23 Jamaica has 28 endangered species (see student book page 271). Research and make notes on what is being done to save one or more of them. Write your answer on a separate sheet of paper.